Waves of
Unleash The Power of

Bartholomeus Nicolaas Engelbertus
Natural Self, Inc

surflifecoach.com

*"Het is altijd wel wat, dan dit, en dan weer dat" * Frans Bauer*

©Bartholomeus Nicolaas Engelbertus 2013 All rights reserved, including the right of reproduction, in whole or in part, in any form.
Published by O N I - Cornwall 2013 ISBN 978-0-9571418-9-6

For

Kiran; my light forever

&

Saba; my breeze of life

&

Those I Love; I will always be what you want,

and more

A personal growth story originating from the time I nearly died.

While surfing the epic North Shore waves of Hawaii a freak wave loomed out of the vast deep blue.

Trapped, and with no way out, tons of oceanic power unleashed itself on me. Tumbling, deep under water and surrounded in bubbly white and grey fizz, oxygen ran out.

Sheer panic, surrender, followed by serene peace.

Floating in light blue, image by happy image, the joyful moments of life slid by.

An inner smile filled my body with joy, as if to give it its last joyride before death.

And so existence as I knew it ceased.

Out of time, out of life, yet aware and present.

Me, but not embodied.

Aware of now, but nowhere here.

Blackness. . .

Light. . .

. . .

Surfaced, miraculously floating on my board, breathing, crying, laughing, reembodied. . .

The world has never been the same since. . .

Thriving On Change

I used to think it was the water that was moving when waves travel towards shore. Like the ripples created by a stone in a pond, it is the energy of the impact that travels, not the water itself.

What if my body is like water, and I am the wave? How could I be aware, and outside my body that day?

What is it in us, that makes the sense of 'me' intrinsically me?

On a mission to find my answers I read stacks of books, and explored many personal growth philosophies. I found many similarities in the world's religions - and - in well-intended modern self help methodologies. In the end, I found the ancient Eastern wisdom from the Tao, The Tibetan Book of the Dead, and the underpinning principles of Bushido the most valuable to understand the more constant aspect of myself.

However useful, it was not until later, due to a highly unforeseen, unexpected, and a very much undesired life change that I discovered how to cultivate a way of being that benefits from change, even the unpredictable variety.

After smashing into my rock bottom in spectacular fashion, I found my *Natural Self*. With nothing left to hide under, all that was left was my 'me' awareness, similar to my near death experience when I nearly drowned in the high seas of Hawaii. However, there was one significant difference. I now understood how the deeper, more default, naturally inclined kind of self gets muddled up with attachments, and dependencies, on what we do in life.

This misidentification with our roles, or rather the level of dependency for contentment this brings, is the main reason for unnatural stress and unhappiness. In our fast paced society it is no wonder we lose touch with our *Natural Self*. Our busy lives are subjected to continuous change, and our roles change accordingly.

Just like the energy of a wave transfers from water to sound and vibrations when it finally breaks on shore, life does not stop once one environment changes into the next. Each environment resonates with nature's waves of energy, and you are in charge of its frequency. We naturally, and instinctively, know how to adapt our frequency to a change in environment. When I smashed into my epiphany, I knew I had to create a way for people to find this freedom from stress and unhappiness, without having to experience the shock and suffering from undesired change.

In *Waves of Change – Unleash The Power of The Natural Self*, I show how to adapt to changing circumstances by utilising your innate natural selective instinct.

It will show you how to ride life's waves of change, effortlessly and naturally. Come on! . . . Surf'sUp! . . . Life'sOn!

Epitome

Natural selection is a natural evolutionary process that results in the survival and success of individuals or groups best adjusted to their environment. People are both the constant: that which adapts, and the variable: that which is adapted.

On the next few pages you will find a brief introduction to the most important concepts and observational epiphanies at the core of the Natural Self System. We meet, in black and white, some naïve learned behaviours that man has developed to give us strength, rationality and control, but which have eroded our ability to thrive naturally in times of change. The rest of the book explores and explodes these myths, releasing you from their power.

The Natural Self System activates via easy, and fun to do exercises, the power to thrive on change. Simply activate this Natural Power within you and you find yourself making the most out of your circumstances in your career and in your personal life. Change becomes your friend, regardless to whether this change is desired, undesired, predictable, or unpredictable. Unnatural stress is no longer part of your life, and unnatural fears are gone forever.

Weak, Strong, & Thrive.

When you are free from the story in your head of what you think is good for you, random change and adversity will give you more upsides than downsides. This is not the same as; 'What does not kill you makes you stronger,' but more like; 'Thriving on the assassination attempt.'

In a world of opposites it is weak versus strong. Strong comes in two forms; 'picking yourself up and carry on' and 'picking yourself up, evolve, and carry on.' The difference is that 'evolving' means to be open enough to adapt, before simply carrying on. By the means of experimentation, evaluation, and trial-and-error methods.

For this to result in you thriving with more upsides than downsides, you have to be free enough from the status, the idea, the story, and your wants and needs which are attached to the situation you are in. All these things are ideas in your head of what you think is good - for you - or for - your perceived outcome.

There are three interlinked concepts that underpin my Natural Self System. The first states that it is our perception (how we see and experience our career, life, and relationships - how things seem) which rules the way we feel and think about things, and what we subsequently do from that state of mind and emotion.

The second observes that our learned approach of classifying ourselves as weak or strong is dangerously incomplete. Rather than simplified opposites, a trinity of states of perception is much more helpful. Being 'Weak' makes us change disadvantageously, being 'Strong' allows us to endure, but we only truly 'Thrive' as we change advantageously.

The third concept applies this trinity to our way of perception. There can now be three ways of being; one that leaves you weak to random change, one that makes you resilient to random change, and one that makes you thrive on random change.

'Weak' is when you identify with your 'doing.' 'Strong is when you identify with your 'being,' and 'Thrive' is when you are free from both.

Nothing Happens for a Reason

Too often, the process of seeking reason compromises your 'natural readiness' for the unseen, unsaid, and unimagined.

Reason and understanding have the habit of being assigned in retrospect. This backward behaviour is a justification, or assigned feel-good -

or feel-better - factor to something that just happened. It indicates a potential dependency on the valuation of something or someone external. Fair enough, we all enjoy external valuation, just do not rely on it solely (mostly). When you analyse and seek reason to justify and explain events, you have taken the 'out of you view', although not dismissing this to be useful at times of reflection, it carries the risk of standing in your own way of seeing new opportunities.

There is no reason to reason. Joy is in that which is not wordy, joy is that which has no logic or explanation.

Nature is our guide; it creates a wide variety of options continually and organically, evolving and thriving without the need for reason or design.

I describe this state as 'Optionality': allowing space within your choices for the unseen, unsaid and unimagined. It comes from the core of our natural self, at no emotional cost, and is something to be enjoyed - not feared.

You do not intrinsically need reason, understanding or logic, to benefit from something: if, that is, you are willing to embrace optionality.

Nature does not question the origin of light or water, yet it benefits freely. Allow yourself to be free from your rational happiness dependency; continuously and organically select your highest emotional pay-off; and, 'enjoy the ride'.

It is, after all, only natural!

Waves of Change

25   **The Natural Self**
What makes you, intrinsically you

45   **The Natural Self Role Model**
Finding your Natural Self, by yourself

59   **The Essence of The Natural You**
Truly knowing Thyself

67   **People**
Perspective & Reality

75   **People Behave According to How Things Seem**
Why people do things, their way

83   **Are You With Me?**
Inspiring people

93   **Learning the Value of Other People's Perceptions**
How to benefit from 'Listening Language'

111 **A Problem Seen Is a Problem Solved**
A definitive problem solver

Waves of Change

121 Love & Relationships
How to make it work

133 The Three Elements of Relationships
What to do & When to do it

145 How to Have More Upsides
Benefit from change

149 Mind Wandering
How to boost happiness

151 Fear: The Story of What Happens Next
Don't believe everything you think

161 Get Out of Your Own Way
And how to do it fast

165 Eye-Opener & Eye-Closer
Awakening & How to sleep peacefully

173 A Story About a Way
All we have is how we feel about ourself, every single moment

This Book

This book is showing you a way to be free from the idea, the story, the status, and wants and needs. The exercises show how our 'attachments to' and 'identifications with' what we do leaves you vulnerable to change. It shows how evolving like a phoenix rebirth will be everlasting and advantageous in life. The way shown is a 'do-it-your-self' exercise, merely reading it will keep the material intellectual. I strongly suggest you 'do' the exercises so to learn experientially.

The Chinese philosopher Confucius (551bC-479BC) said; *"I hear and I forget, I see and I remember, I do and I understand."* Enough said; it is up to you to 'just read it' - or to 'just do it!'

Once done (understood) correctly the exercises are a personal growth and a post-traumatic-growth experience. With this experience on board, the book introduces you to ways of advantageous outcomes in career, life, and relationships by showing you how to thrive with more upsides than downsides. It will show you that people behave according to how they perceive the situation. It will give you ways of understanding growth. It will show you how to inspire others, how to change default futures, how to resolve meaninglessness, how to communicate, how to inspire yourself and others to find your own answers, how to emerge your own leadership, and how to empower your own responsibility.

As I am writing this introduction (before I endeavour turning my notes into a book) I will quickly take the opportunity to outline that my writing is never meant to be an intellectual piece of work; there are far more academically minded folk out there who can write volumes of text, repeating a simple concept in many eloquent and elegant ways. I am a Dutchman writing in English: I am sure my culture and heritage will shine through at times.

I intend to write a simple guidebook, cutting to the chase, avoiding endless repetition. I also avoid the common personal growth book format of providing real world examples of people and companies I have worked with. Because my perception of what happened when I worked with Royalty, British Special Forces folk, global medical firm leadership, and Joe-Junky homeless dude is simply not important.

This book is here to show you a way of being free from 'prediction of' - and 'preparation for' the future. Stories would only suggest some misguided status of author-authority (and I am you, nothing more - nothing less). Of course it is more important to be ready for the unexpected than it is to be primed by suggesting what could happen should you find yourself in similar situations to my examples.

Once Again: Nothing happens for a reason. Reason is a post event attempt to find mental comfort by assigning the 'why's' to the 'what's'. Even though this is perfectly human, please be free from the assumption that similar indicators will result in the same outcomes. We all do this but try to leave some space for the unexpected. We truly build our own prisons.

Free yourself from this kind of thinking by being 'open to' - and 'ready for' - other outcomes you may not have associated with these events before. Nature survives on this free way of being - it is our natural state to thrive like this.

I call it our *Natural Self*.

The Natural Self

When we consider ourselves to be part of nature (and I fully appreciate some folk do not) we may learn a thing or two about evolution. Nature has the beautiful ability to self regulate by mutation, natural selection, and genetic drift. Stormy seas go from chaos to self organised sets of waves traveling to the edges of the ocean.

Change and pressures of changing environments cause adaptations in the structure of being, with the intention to survive, and to a certain extent, self heal. Every time our immune system successfully overcomes an infection we become stronger - as we have adapted. Whole systems adjust as each integral aspect tinkers and tweaks according to its environmental random stimulus. If there is a constant in nature it is trial and error, keep what works, ditch what does not. To thrive one would be - as a rule of thumb - be advised to do the same, and do so with a mind open enough, and a heart unattached enough, to allow for the previously unseen to potentially become reality. Humankind and its profound ability to emotionally invest in a person, idea, or object, could become a victim of its investments when the emotional dependence to external happiness, joy, and contentment overshadows a person's ability to access his or her own innate source of contentment. The natural self is the gateway to the unlimited source of contentment. The clarity of this gateway depends heavily on how similar your present - or dominant - way of being is to your natural self inclined preferences, values, and tendencies.

We often see ourselves as the sum of our collective identities, all correlating to their unique set of circumstances. With 'identities,' I mean our roles in life. In my humble existence this means I see myself as the total of being a man, father, surfer, personal growth coach, martial artist, friend, spouse, family member, neighbour, Dutchman, and so forth. In time and through experience we expand and build on our attributes, only adding to the complexity of our identity and the way we perceive our world accordingly. In our collective of identities, our 'system of self,' each integral identity role can tweak and tinker according to the ever changing input of its environment. On this level change is little and easy. It is all about having the clarity of mind to be present enough and open enough to new opportunity. The key is to continuously evaluate and reevaluate without buying into the assumption that we know what will happen next based on past events/experience. For this to work, we have to understand our collective of roles and see how we have created our ways of being in each of its unique circumstances.

Naturally we adapt to each of our role's circumstances with the intention to survive. Before we start seeking to understand our own collective, let's first look at the third concept I introduced earlier. The concept where our perception is a trinity - a group of three ways of being; one that leaves you weak to random change, one that makes you resilient to random change, and one that makes you thrive on random change. 'Weak' is when you identify with your 'doing'. 'Strong is when you identify with your 'being', and 'Thrive' is when you are free from both.

Weak means subjected to random change, where change seems a disadvantage, and mostly identified with doing. The weak role is the part of you that identifies with what you do, and whom you seem to be. Here you are (too much) identified with your status, your actions, and relationship status. It creates feel-good dependency. This 'being too identified with what you do' often comes out in self expression and social rules. What is the most common question asked socially when meeting a new person? After we learn the persons name we either are introduced to, or ask about, what this person 'does'(for a living). Most of us answer something like this - I will use my own circumstances - fill in the assigned statuses with your own - : "I am a personal growth trainer, father of two, surfer and bujutsu martial artist." I push the boat out a bit here of course. Usually a person mentions what seems appropriate to the social circumstances we are in. In a professional setting we probably focus on our professional status, and in a more informal setting we may expand on our family / relationship status and personal interests. When we dig a little deeper we find attributes like characteristics and beliefs; "I am a go-getter who perseveres until I have what I want"

- or - "I am a loving and accepting kind of person, only seeing the best in others." Interestingly enough, each of our named life areas is a role identity label that changes according to its environment. The role identity and its context depend on, and get affected by, each other. They correlate to be precise. Just like how our parental role changes according to our children's needs as they grow older (parenting style and ways change from babyhood to teenager), our professional side has adapted to work circumstances, our relationship self has adapted to changes in your partner or partnership. Because these aspects of us correlate to change I call them 'roles' - as it is something we 'do' - however close to the heart our roles may feel to us. These roles are not weak by default, they become weak when we identify with them too much. When you know your deeper more permanent self clearly, you have become less attached to your roles (The Strong Self). Any unwanted change or adversity has a lesser effect on how you think and feel about yourself - leaving you clearer to see opportunities once missed - as you took things too personally by blindly focussing on the idea in your mind of 'what you think is good for you.' So only with the power of 'knowing thyself' you can cultivate a way of being where you no longer depend on your roles (and others) for feeling good.

Imagine what that does to your attachments to outcomes? Indeed; you will have a lot more emotional and intellectual bandwidth to focus on what is really happening moment by moment. With such presence, you see new angles and ways, and you find you have the peace and clarity of mind to adjust to any new, or unexpected, developments. This way of being thrives in times of change and adversity (The Natural Self).

It is in our deepest essence, our genes and instinct, to evolve. Just like nature we tweak and adjust, modify and mutate. We do so according to our environment, or the way we perceive our environment to be. When you mostly identify with your roles, and have emotionally invested in them you are bound to tweak, modify, adjust, and evolve from the context of the role. This builds stronger attachments to the roles and you will feel more and more identified with this mixed bag of roles - as opposed to being a someone who 'does' these things. Identified with your mixed bag of roles, tweaked and evolved in time, we become less flexible to perceive our environments in a free and open way. Increasingly we will only see what we expect to see, and that is formed through years of emotional investment in who you think you are. As most people have many roles in our busy lives, this way of being is like keeping all your characters moving like spinning plates. Most of your energy and awareness is focussed on doing this, and you are overloaded with stimuli. Obviously a person's attention cannot be focussed on everything, and therefore, one perceives their environment through filters of expectation. However, you can appreciate that the busier your attention is, the less perceptual bandwidth you will have to notice the new, and the changed.

When I speak of perceiving, or perception, I mean this in the broadest sense of the word; visually, mentally, emotionally, instinctively, and energetically.

This concept of filtering and bandwidth of perception is best explained by taking the visual perception as an example. Visually there is something known as 'inattentional' or 'perceptual blindness': a failure to notice an unexpected stimulus that is in plain sight.

Even though anticipation and expectation are generally a good thing, when the mind is overloaded we become less capable to see the unexpected, and are therefore less capable to adjust appropriately. The most famous experiment is the invisible gorilla test, and if you have not seen it already, find the video's on youtube. And we all know that being on your cell/mobile phone takes up a certain amount of your perception bandwidth, right?

When most of our perception bandwidth, in the broadest sense of the word, is taken up by being too identified with your roles in life, you have less time to be in that zone of contentment that is your real, deeper, more default, naturally inclined kind of self. There is simply less bandwidth available to experience self generated happiness, contentment, and love. Now imagine what that state of being does to your work performance, your physical wellbeing, and your relationships?

No wonder we, at some point, will rely more on externally provided happiness, love, and contentment, as this is where most of the bandwidth is at. You obviously try to avoid change to, or anything that has an impact on, your source of contentment. This is what builds the dependency.

How do you know if you are too identified with your roles or depend too much on others and your statuses to feel good? Simple: The effect of sudden unexpected change will have more downsides than upsides. In our natural state (our natural self) we have most perceptual bandwidth on our own source of contentment. I am not talking about being in altered or enlightened states of mind. Note that I say; 'most' of our perceptual bandwidth, as to live life successfully you have to assign your awareness to your work, your leisure activities, your people, and your relationships.

The external joy this provides is like oil on your self generated contentment-fire. Any external headwind you may experience feeds your ability to learn and self repair. The natural self is like having a strong clear channel and flow through your internal perceptual bandwidth with degrees of awareness invested in your external life. Being like this is who we are naturally. Individuality comes with preferences, and perhaps even tendencies, cultivated in early childhood. However, knowing yourself this deeply can enhance your ability to create a happy and fulfilling existence in all our life areas. It is a fine art to be unattached enough to your role statuses without losing sight of your deepest preferences and desires.

As we are hardwired to evolve, we will evolve from whatever we identify with. In other words, we evolve our roles as well as our strong deeper self and our natural self. When change is pleasant, or not too unpleasant to our role self, we may become unaware of our attachments to its circumstances. When unwanted change appears either suddenly by imperceptible shifts, or by catastrophic rare events, we incapacitate ourselves to act swiftly and promptly to benefit from this opportunity. Let's not forget the vast amount of emotional energy it takes to deal with negative change when we take our roles (too) personally. This requires processing (brain/mind) power, and all this energy spent on dealing with the impact on our quality of thoughts and emotions cannot be used to see new opportunity, chance, and perspective.

In nature, the demise (to a certain extent) of one is the benefit of the other and next. In the animal kingdom the fittest and strongest survive by means of mating rituals. Nature carries on adapting to its environment. The inevitable change becomes its requirement for survival. From the perspective of nature, weakness in an aspect makes the whole stronger. The roles in our life are the expression of our natural self. Just in case you may perceive roles to be bad, wrong, or unhelpful, I better reinforce the joy of roles and how wonderful, good, and useful they are. We evolve our roles, and we can do this from the perspective of being identified with our deeper authentic strong self, making the whole expression of ourself Natural. The natural self is therefore a collective of selves where the demise of a role part is beneficial. It enables the nature of us (the natural self) to reinvent, self heal, and self generate, a new version (or a new role altogether) that performs better in its context; hence allows our whole being to thrive. When you are too identified with a role, or part of, you are going to fight to keep (it) alive, just as it is, and so slowing down - postponing the inevitable adaptation that the new circumstances require. We all know how devastating one role can be to the experience of the other ones. How does maintaining a horrible relationship affect your work and your leisure life? How does a horrible work environment affect your personal, and leisure life?

When you know you are not your role, or you are no longer mostly depending on it for feeling good, it becomes easy to let go of the idea, the status, and that external source of contentment, when it no longer serves the greater good of your whole self. Remember; only when you no longer need/depend on your role to feel good, you are capable of thriving in that role.

My perception of the world is that there is nothing to fix, things are as they are, and looking back is mostly reinforcing the past. So the exercise that follows is not designed to fix anything, or to make 'wrong' 'right'. There is no such thing, only thinking makes it so.

"There is nothing either good or bad, but thinking makes it so" - William Shakespeare - Hamlet.

First we will look at your roles in life and create some clarity around that. The easiest way to start is to look at three life areas; your 'personal life,' your 'professional life,' and your 'leisure life.' To understand what is a role let's define it as a part of you that correlates to its changing environment. So change to that part of you happens hand in hand to its direct context. Parent roles change as the child's needs change, work roles change when a new task is introduced, and with more experience your leisure role changes. A role is therefore; a part of you that has a label, like parent, husband, wife, girlfriend, business person, job-title, leisure activity name, etc.

Let's start with thinking of what is the most important personal relationship role, most important professional role, and most important leisure role. Remember these guidelines are here to get started, you can always come back and work on other roles later. If you have more than one role in a category that feels very important, pick one that you want to have your intended outcome for the most - the one where, what you want from it, has the most riding on it. The best way of doing this exercise is by using pen and paper. Different colours, sheets of A4 paper or, at the very least, a notebook and pen. If you want to do it all in your head, and even though I am sure you find great insights, the results are always better when you externalise by writing your answers down. This frees up your bandwidth for each subsequent part of the process, it will simply enhance and deepen your learning experience.

If taking yourself through a personal growth process like this is a bit daunting, relax in the knowing that doing the exercise as designed - this means; using pen and paper - will only make things better. If you find yourself hungry for more, come back to the role model exercise with more aspects of roles, or more roles, after finishing the book - or go on a personal growth adventure by attending one of the *Surf Life Coach Natural Self Sessions or Retreats.*

For now, we start your intrinsic adventure with the role model exercise. So find your notepad, pens, and/or sheets of paper, some time and space, and let's go!

"Imagination is more important than knowledge"
Albert Einstein- Physicist (1879 - 1955)

The Natural Self Role Model

Earlier I asked you to think of the most important personal relationship role, most important professional role, and most important leisure role.

Take a sheet of paper for each and label each role-sheet with its name. For example; 'Team Leader,' 'Wife,' 'Outdoors Person.'

Place these sheets in the space around you and take up a position that feels comfortable (in the sense of feeling most at ease, relaxed, and just you).

This is a space that 'feels right,' while you think of what the most important CHARACTERISTICS for each particular role are.

WRITE the characteristics on the role-sheet. Address ONE ROLE AT THE TIME.

When you have done one, move on to the next.

Once each role has its characteristics listed PLACE them back in the space around you.

Return to your comfortable space.

Focus on one role's characteristics and determine WHAT KIND OF CHARACTERISTICS they are.

For example; if one of the characteristics is 'strong' then ask yourself 'What kind of strong is that?' The answer could be something like; 'A psychological - well balanced kind of strong.'

Note down whatever comes up, no one is going to mark your paper, and the more you go with your 'first' answer the better. Write this on your sheet. Address each characteristic of each role like this.

NEEDS: Return to your comfortable space and address one role at the time when you assign the role's needs. Needs are 'something wanted' or 'required' and 'deemed essential' or 'very important.'

Assign, and record on the corresponding role-sheet, each role's NEEDS first.

Then return to your comfortable space and ask yourself, gently; 'What kind of need is that?' Write the answer on the role-sheet.

Do this for each need, one role at the time.

Once you have done this do the same for the following attributes:

TOOLS/SKILLS: Tools/Skills in the context of this exercise, are things used to achieve the role's purpose, such as people (for example; staff, family or friends) or devices and learning that are created by a human being. These can be systems, things and tricks.

One role at the time, list the tools/skills first for each role, followed by 'What kind of tool/skill is that?'

Write all answers on the sheet - attach extra sheets if required.

Return to your comfortable zone/space.

RIGHTS/OBLIGATIONS: Rights/Obligations are the authority and course of action to which a person is morally, culturally, or legally bound. For some roles you may find more 'Rights,' for some you may find more 'Obligations,' and for some roles you may have answers for both. The idea is to use the answer which sprang to mind first and go with that.

Do one role at the time, list the rights/obligations for each role, followed by 'What kind of right/obligation is that?'

Write all answers on the sheet - attach extra sheets if required.

And, return to your comfortable space again.

BEHAVIOUR/ACTIONS: List the specific kinds of behaviour and/or actions that go with that role. If you notice you are assigning a value to that (judging it in some way) you can already specify the 'What kind' part of the exercise.

Once more; one role at the time, list the behaviour/actions first for each role, followed by 'What kind of behaviour/action is that?'

Write all answers on the sheet - attach extra sheets if required.

Go back to your comfortable space.

By looking at your roles like this we are slowly starting to untangle your life areas, assign value, and so reevaluate your attributes. You may see that some roles are closer to 'you' and some are a bit more foreign. It is not important how close or far they are, it just requires you to know so you can adjust accordingly.

To add to the clarity we are now going to focus on the kind of environment your role mostly inhabits. To assist you in assigning the right context, the next part of the exercise contains a list of keywords. For best results place your role somewhere in the space around you - this may be in the same or another space.

The point is to place them in the right space in relation to your comfort space. Have a play with this, place them in different spaces and see how you feel. You will see that there is a 'zone' where the role appears to be in the 'right' space, distance, and angle, to your comfort zone.

Once you have placed the role in the 'right' space, go and 'be the role' in that role-space. Take a pen and extra paper if required and use the following questions (from the perspective of the role space you occupy) to get a sense of the things that create its environment:

When you picture yourself in that role's space, are you;

...Inside or Outside?

...Are there Objects?

...Are there other People?

...What Colors are there?

...Is it Bright or is it Dim?

...Is there a Smell?

...What is Happening?

...Is there a Sensation?

...Is there a Feeling?

...Is there an Emotion?

What kind of world is that world?

Take a moment to get a sense of what kind of knowledge this role has. Ensure you capture this on your role sheet. You can write, draw, or represent it in any other way, should you feel that is more appropriate.

Repeat this for the two other roles.

Place them in the right space, go there, feel into the role, be it, and answer the questions from its perspective.

Go to your comfortable zone and take some time to observe each role and notice what aspects of the role's world are similar, and where the differences are.

In each role there have been defining moments, moments that have shaped the role to be what they are right now. Whether you deem these defining moments positive or not is not important, it is important however, to go with whatever defining moments you thought of first. It just paints a clearer picture of your roles, and therefore, will make your result better.

Notice any tendencies to 'flower up' - make look

better - any of your answers; it may just belong to that role you are working on at the time.

For each role note down three defining moments. Describe how the role changed from the time before the defining moment and how you perceived that defining moment at the time.

Do this for each role, from the perspective of your comfortable space zone.

Take a new sheet of paper and define, describe, and evaluate, your comfortable space. How does it feel, and what is it like? What kind of thoughts do you experience?

Now look at each role and compare them to your comfortable space.

What in the role is similar to you?

What in that role is unlike your comfortable space experience?

Write, draw, and/or represent this on a separate sheet of paper (one per role) and add this to your comfortable space description.

Now physically leave your comfortable space and move about in the space where your roles and comfortable zone spaces are. You can crawl, walk, skip, and dance, as long as you flow through the area. Notice any characteristics, needs, tools, skills, rights, obligations, behaviours, and actions, that are similar between all spaces. See those that are not. Are any of these transferable from role to role? And if so, how?

If you see an attribute you want to transfer, write it on a piece of paper or post-it note and walk it from one role to the other. Deliver it to the other role. Imagine how this role would adapt such an attribute.

Notice how some attributes originated from one role but transferred to another role as if they contaminated it. Break these contaminations by crossing out the attribute from one role, write it on a post-it or piece of paper and deliver it to the role it originated from.

Notice how you perceive some of the attributes in a positive or negative way. Perhaps some attributes are positive for one role, but not so good for the next? Note down anything you wish to change by making a role specific 'change sheet' (write, draw, and/or represent these changes).

Attach it to its corresponding role. When you feel complete and satisfied you have 'put your world to rights' go back to your comfortable zone space.

Take a few moments to reflect on all this.

The Essence of The Natural You

The essence of the natural you is the multi dimensional melting pot of attributes and preferences. Without it, you wouldn't be you. The intrinsic that was, is and will be; it is 'that' within you that makes you, you. 'That' which was present from your early years, throughout life, to where you are now.

The essence is 'that' which does not depend on others for being what it is. This also clarifies what is a 'role' aspect of self; 'that' which depends on others for being what it is. Also note that your natural essence is therefor not: 'life', 'soul', 'awareness', 'consciousness', 'the all', 'spirit', 'void', 'love', 'light', and so forth. All these are present in everyone, regardless of how we label and see this in our own life.

Take a new sheet of paper and describe the attributes of the natural you by the means of naming each attribute.

Expand by asking yourself; 'What kind of Attribute is that?'

Now describe what preferences the natural you has:

...What kind of environment is preferred?

...What type of people?

...How do these people behave?

...What type of activities do you prefer?

...Is there a preference to lead?

...Or to follow?

...A preference for detail?

...Or the overview?

...For a careful evaluation of options?

...Or a jumping in the deep end approach?

...For being introverted or extroverted?

And,...when you look at these preferences, what is it like when all these preferences are there?

How do your natural attributes and preferences compare to your personal, professional, and leisure roles?

When areas of our roles match, or mostly match our natural self, things are effortless. Whatever it is in that role; you are happy to do that until the cows come home, any time, happy days! The level of similarity sets the level of effortlessness. The part which is unmatched feels hard, difficult, and will require effort.

With the clarity of knowing your natural self better, most people clearly see why certain aspects of their personal and professional roles are more challenging than others. Adapting to something you can clearly identify as not matching your natural self sufficiently is super precise personal growth.

Because we now know that feeling out of sync is down to a mismatch of preferential circumstances, it is easier to adapt. You do not need to change your preferences, you just need to know it is your preferences that signal the out-of-sync-ness by firing off an emotional response (usually a discomfort of some kind).

It is amazing to see how just knowing this will alleviate the discomfort experienced, freeing emotional and mental bandwidth energy to form a positive response. Problem named is sometimes problem solved. Facing the problem is making space for solving it.

Note that the context of the role dictates the how 'in sync' the natural self is in that role. Take your professional role for instance. Within that role you will have a range of circumstances that dictate how you experience that role. Just the presence of one person can fundamentally shift this. The presence of one person, or the introduction of a new person, may shift how introvert or extrovert the role becomes, or how much leadership and initiative you show. It is important to understand that the role correlates to each shift and change in its environment, and that it does so according to how this role has evolved in that context until now. The more that role has evolved separately from the deeper natural self, the more reliant it is on its context (to survive).

Another good reason to mostly bring yourself to your role. As all involved are also in their roles and therefore subject to the law of correlation, a change in the way you act out your role will change the way they act out theirs. The key is to have clarity what in the environments of your roles is in-sync, and what is out-of-sync, with your naturally inclined preferences.

Define the three most important contexts in each role, and notice how synced the natural self is in those contexts.

Compare the contexts within each role and notice the factors that make the difference.

What kind of thinking, and what kind of behaviour, would suit you in those circumstances?

If you have identified a significant challenge to overcome; describe the challenge and how it seems from your perspective now. Make a note of it, you can use this later in the book when we look at overcoming obstacles.

Explore more roles to deepen your connection to your natural self state. You can also explore one role and identify the three most important sub-roles this role has. This could be particularly useful in your professional role. You may see patterns and similar aspects in other yet unexplored roles. You may see a link in defining moments and certain kind of behaviours.

Exploring more roles will further clarify your natural self state, and will make it easier to stay present in it.

The most important thing is that you now have more clarity about your deeper authentic preferences.

You probably recognise that this is your default kind of self, a very stable sense of self. This is the part of you that can handle any kind of change.

People

Understanding a person's perception is an impossibility. Empathy goes a long way, but you still use your own perspective to qualify the other person's point of view. Use your empathic nature to acknowledge people, their words, actions, and presence. Acknowledge them simply up to the point of "I see you." Accept people as they are, however, this does not mean you have to accept their actions should they cross your preferential values. You can never see from a person's perspective as this perspective is unique, just like yours. It has formed over years of life experience of, and exposure to, one's individual environment. Mix in a person's own unique array of roles and the degree to which they identify with their roles, and add to that the context that has formed the role to be what it is, and you may start to see it is simply impossible to have the same experience from another person's perspective. We may have an 'educated and well informed guess' based on the familiarity and time spend with this particular person, and we may both call the cushion red, but it may be green to my eyes.

So where is the common ground? The common ground is calling the cushion red. I assume you see what I see, you do the same, and now we both feel safe. We have created a shared reality. A shared reality is the assumption that the other person is understanding things in a similar way. This puts an interesting perspective on the concept of truth. Is truth the shared reality, or is truth the individual's perspective of that? As we can only assume what the other perspective(s) may be, truth as a concept can only be assumed.

There is no truth, there is only perspective. Reality is the experience of the perspective, this is what makes the shared reality so important.

A shared reality, the assumed alignments of individual perspectives, gives us a sense of belonging, purpose, and well-being. It is extremely unnerving to a human being to have a misaligned perspective to a commonly shared reality of others. Perceiving something most people do not, can isolate a person and ignite emotional responses related to being able to trust their own, and other people's perspectives. Without a reality to share nothing can be trusted. This is what feeds cultural differences. As individual perspectives encountering a new place (work, city/countryside, new country, culture, or social group) we automatically adapt our perspective to what seems to be the shared reality, in order to fit in. We do this naturally because this way we have a greater chance of survival in that particular environment. This is nature's way. The environment dictates how life manifests itself.

A tree grows with the main wind direction. A river runs according to the landscape. People form shared realities according to previously created shared realities of others in their environment of influence.

Hence why different cultures have different emotional and cognitive responses to the same stimulus. I remember my first trip to Japan many years ago. I learned very quickly one does not walk over tatami while wearing shoes. One puts on slippers to enter the toilet facilities and does not walk out back to your table in the restaurant still wearing those toilet slippers. OK, it provided hilarious entertainment to the hundred or so restaurant punters, but simultaneously it may have inspired ideas of how to make the social rules more understandable to foreign visitors. 'The do's and do-not's of the slippers and the bathroom.'

You may sense 'a breach' of your cultural values when a person with a different social environment to yours behaves differently to you. What a word means to you comes down to rational and analytical interpretation. How you react to it emotionally, depends on your shared realities.

We build our shared realities with more than words. It is the intention, the deeper preferences, values, and instincts that we perceive in the communication and presence of others. The level of your openness to understanding the deeper intention of people's behaviour influences how well you are able to pick up changes in their attitude.

People's perspective drives why they are doing things that way. How you perceive this will determine how well you adapt to (unexpected) change.

How swiftly can you adapt your perspective to align yourself with the new shared reality to benefit from the new context? Tip of the day; the more resistance you feel, the more you have identified with this perspective. How much of this perspective is naturally yours, and how much of this perspective have you formed to make a life role fit in its environment?

Remember the art is to enhance your career, life, and leisure roles, not to discard them. Do not depend on your roles for feeling good, feeling good comes from your strong self, the authentic deeper naturally inclined sense of self. Enjoy your roles from there, let the external joy be the oil on your own fire, so life is hotter and lighter altogether.

Know that alone, you are perspective, with others you are reality.

Know that people behave according to their perspective, regardless whether this perspective is mostly their natural self perspective, or their role-perspective. It is totally irrelevant to understand this in another person as there are many factors that influence how a person behaves. While in personal relationships it is useful to know your partner's deeper values and preferences, it remains pointless to know what behaviour in others is more role driven, and what is more natural self driven.

There is one thing that is undeniable though; people behave according to how things seem to them in the moment.

People Behave According to How Things Seem.

With 'behaviour,' I mean behaviour in the broadest sense of the word, behaviour in action and deed, as well as, 'that' which is communicated physically, kinesthetically, intentionally, and unintentionally. However much people's behaviour is a representation of their authentic natural self or their investment in, and dependency on their roles, is not important. All you need to know is they respond according to how things seem to them. This will be according to their shared reality, that is why people from similar backgrounds and similar cultures living in similar times seem to respond in a similar way. A fairly safe rule of thumb, should you not discard that individual perspectives may differ, and create a tipping point that shifts the group's response.

Remember that your roles change as new people or new circumstances are present. Change happens gradually, step by step, imperceptible, and appears suddenly. Be ready for that at all times because gradual change is imperceptible until it reaches the tipping point. Then it appears, from our point of view, suddenly. All of a sudden the grass of your lawn appears too long. That did not happen overnight, it simply passed a tipping point. Now it seems too long to you, sparking a response. You go out and mow the lawn, or ask someone to do it for you. Your behaviour is driven by how things seem to you.

Your child all of a sudden seems to have a more grown up perspective and opinion. Guess what, that didn't happen overnight. It just seems different from your perspective because you observed your child differently. So you adapt your behaviour accordingly. Same counts for people in general, all of a sudden a person or a group appears different to you. You got it, that didn't happen overnight either!

Whether you are a leader or an individual in a group, if you desire change and aspire change you have to remember the golden rule: People respond better to 'why you do' things, than to 'what you are doing.' Remember we build our shared realities with more than words. It is the intention, the deeper preferences, values, and instincts that we perceive in the communication of others. Simply being in the same space allows us to sense each other's presence like this.

From a natural perspective; it is how we feel about things that drives our behaviour. This is fundamental biology, not psychology. Our newest part of the brain in evolutionary terms is the neocortex.

It is this part of the brain, which interestingly enough is the outer part of the brain physically, that is responsible for our rational and analytical thought and language. The inner part of the brain, our limbic brain, is responsible for all our feelings like trust and loyalty. It drives our behaviour, all decision making, and it has no capacity for language. Hence people respond to why you do things and not what you do. The 'why' is something that people sense and feel. When this value driven intent is similar to our natural preferences and values we experience a sense of trust and loyalty.

From an evolutionary perspective, it is this type of environment which makes survival and thriving more likely. This is why 'how people feel about things' determines decision making and behaviour. All the reasoning, facts and figures will not motivate people to buy into what you represent. It has to feel right, because our limbic brain responds like that, without words, without analytics. People make decisions that seem to contradict their own analysed rational thought. Simply because it does not feel right. The gut feeling. The instinct. The reason why you do things is driven by your natural self, your deeper authentic strong essence (that which makes you, you; that which does not depend on others for being what it is).

People respond to how things seem to them, and respond mostly to 'why' you do things, and not to 'what' you do. So if you aspire change, come from the authentic natural strong essence of self. Align your words with the instinctive communication of feelings and vibes, the energy you radiate. Communicate WHY you are saying what you are saying, WHY you are doing what you are doing, and WHY you are feeling what you are feeling.

In other words; show up in your roles as your natural self, circumstance permitting. If you are a leader then show up completely, and if your role's circumstances are somewhat more limited, show up to the degree deemed possible.

Now you know your Natural Self better you have a clearer line of communication to your deeper instincts. Like our limbic brain reflects; this part of you has no language, just sensations. In order to do the right thing for you, you need to be clear on your natural preferences and essence. This way you can relate to the external world via your role interface without losing the wisdom of your natural instincts. Start with listening to your instincts, and then follow your instincts to the degree possible in your role's context.

In personal relationships you will have much more bandwidth for obeying your natural instincts than in any professional context - unless you are the chief, chair, and core of the organisation of course. Human beings have a strong sense of what we communicate, and equally what we do not communicate. The more you align your communication with your natural self, the deeper the impact you have on the reality shared with other people.

People behave according to how things seem. People also do not notice change. Change happens imperceptibly, gradually, then appears suddenly. So, do not expect results of your change suddenly, the outside world is blind to it - remember the inattentional blindness gorilla? The world is blind to your change in communication, intention, and aspirations, until the shared reality reaches the tipping point from their perspective. Only then there will be a change in their behaviour: because people act according to how things seem.

Are You With Me?

People respond to 'why.' 'Why' always has a future implication. Being with a person or a group means the shared reality of their deeper preferences and values has a future which will reflect that. If nothing would change in the shared reality, you would be able to predict the future fairly accurately as people's behaviour correlates to how things seem. To what extent this is true, depends on how dependent the person and the group are on keeping their environment the same. Shared realities can be kept alive artificially for quite some time. From relationships where both partners are no longer that well connected (and pretend to themselves they are), to a global economic system where governments keep bailing out banks and whole countries. When at last the tipping point of change shifts the reality, the impact is often perceived as devastating.

I guess you have your own relationship story that reflects this (I certainly do). The global financial crisis is instigated by an economic model of everlasting growth. In other words: a model that does not allow for random stressors. In nature random stress often finds a beautiful pattern of equilibrium. Just think of intense storms that turn wild, chaotic seas into a pattern of waves that travel through the ocean in organised lines until they meet their shores of change. Throw a rock in a still pond and watch how nature adjusts and finds a new balance.

Folk doodling along the shoreline, too busy not noticing the change in wave size, may just be caught out by a rogue wave. Change is never devastating to those who align their natural deeper values - as emotional wellbeing is not linked to things staying the same. Because their happiness and contentment does not rely on what has changed, they cope much better with change of any kind. The clearer we are about our own 'why's' and the clearer our personal and professional partners are about theirs, the easier it is to be aligned in the journey. When people come together in shared beliefs, preferences, and values, the stronger the bond is: and the stronger these collaborations are.

Imagine the leadership of a clothing company communicating to its employees: "We will change our supplier requirements to working with environmentally responsible eco friendly suppliers. From now on we will only use organic and recycled materials. We do this because we care about our planet and our children. We do this because this responsible way of doing business contributes to a better future. We are really happy with this change.

Let's tell our customers why we are changing our supply chain, and make them feel happy too."

People respond to why; hence it is those that agree with your 'why' who become part of that change. In fact; there is no need to motivate or to have incentives because when people respond on a 'feel good' level they feed their deeper compelling drive, their modus operandi, which results in feeling contented. If the employees of this clothing company would not feel that they are part of this move towards a better future, and subsequent better quality of life for the greater good, there would be much less buy-in. The sales team may just not get the 'why' across to the customer and speak of the organic, eco-friendly material as a more expensive marketing gimmick rather than the deeper values of the company. People make decisions based on how they feel about something. How they feel about something, comes from how things seem to them. Hence the vital thing in team development is the alignment of 'the why's.' Successful partnerships and collaborations have one thing in common; a shared passion. People easily learn and adapt skills but resist changing their values and preferences. When you communicate your passion and why you are doing all this, people buy into what you stand for, and use the rational analytical as a language to reinforce why they are feeling good for getting involved. Try doing that from a role you are mostly out-of-sync with. Boom! Some of you have now figured out why something in their professional life is not working. Those personal life things? Stay with me, I will come to that later.

There is no such thing as inconsequential communication. There is no such thing as a throwaway comment. There is no such thing as a trivial remark. What may seem unimportant to you may be perceived in a way that drastically affects the lives of others. Words, like thoughts, are the seeds of emotional responses, and subsequent behaviour.

There is an Arabic proverb that says; *'Do not speak if your words do not improve on the beauty of silence.'* Let's just expand that to communication in general and: *'Do not communicate with language, body language, and intention, if it does not improve on the silence.'*

You are responsible for the feelings you leave behind in others. Everything you do will affect others. I am not saying we should all become a Dalai Lama clone and preach compassion and love all the time. Why not start by being aware of your emotional trail and remember; people behave according to how things seem.

Speak not from the perspective of the past if you desire change. Speak from your heart, your why, and involve those who are part of that journey. Look ahead, speak in 'WE,' not 'I.' 'We' is 'truer' to an aligned shared reality. People feel a 'we' and think an 'I.' 'We' creates loyalty and trust among those of similar natural self preferences and values. Use directional momentum in your language. Share in your goals and aspirations. Make it a shared future so it sets the direction and tone of the step by step change.

Ensure the idea and possibility of which you speak do not become a source of contentment. This is the difference between talking and thinking about it, and actually doing it. People feed of the idea or the possibility that it may happen, and rather than working towards that, settle for the feel-good factor this kind of thinking already brings.

This is why it is vital not to identify with your roles to the extent that your happiness mostly depends on it. Stay rooted in your natural self, know that the external brings temporary joy, not lasting joy. So do not rely on it.

Dream big and face the reality of where you are today. Rest in the knowing that you do not need your dream to become reality in order to feel good. You already are content. Be humble and acknowledge the present circumstances. Only by not relying on your dreams for happiness are you free. Without this dependency you are giving yourself a thriving chance not to get stuck in a nightmare. If you lead a company, group, or organisation, be very aware of this in your team. This is another good reason to encourage your people to show up in their role as their natural self. Not only will their increased emotional and attentional bandwidth give better results, you will also get there faster - as they are less depended on the idea of how to achieve the goal. As the core of the group, you have the extraordinary task of staying grounded in reality while striving and thriving towards change.

To recap; people make decisions based on how they feel about it. How they feel about it, depends on what you communicate from your intention, the 'why.' The clearer you are on 'why you are doing this, want this, aspire this,' the clearer your overall communication is. Know where you want to go, and know who you want to join you on that journey. Involve them by communicating with the future in mind. Speak from 'we' and not 'I.' Be aware of how you say things because you are responsible for the feeling you leave behind in others.

And, never lose touch of reality by letting the joy of the dream be sufficient.

Learning The Value of Other People's Perceptions

When you come from your natural self, and you enjoy the pleasure of self generated and self reliant happiness, you truly understand silence.

Your roles have stories to tell, and you speak with passion (why you are going there), engage others (who is joining your journey), and relay information only if it improves the greater good of the shared reality.

The shared reality is by its very nature a creation of individual perspectives. Although we may never be able to truly experience another person's perspective we can do a lot to get a close sense of their point of view.

To do this successfully we must communicate with little preconception.

Leo Lev Nikolayevich Tolstoy (Russian writer, and moral thinker; 1828 - 1910) said; *"The most difficult subjects can be explained to the most slowwitted man if he has not formed any idea of them already, but the simplest thing cannot be made clear to the most intelligent man if he is firmly persuaded that he knows already, without a shadow of a doubt, what is laid before him."*

Have a *free conversation mindset:* To truly hear people you have to be free from the dependency on your internal expert, consultant, helper, and saviour roles. Even if you are in a specific role situation like being at work, be more present as your natural self during a conversation. This way you have the clearest connection to your instinctive receiver.

Empty you mind of preconceptions and resist the urge to overrule someone's ideas with your own. Do not make suggestions, or interrupt someone by interjecting your solution or idea.

Give someone 100% of your attention and encourage your conversation partner to speak freely. Remember to be aware of your emotional trail, so when you invite someone to speak freely do not hold their perspectives against them. They will never speak from their truth again if you do so.

Before you engage in an open and honest conversation; a meaningful conversation; ensure you are in your *'free conversation mindset'* as described above. Make sure you have the time and have avoided potential distractions. Turn that phone off! If you can't (really?) and you have this conversation over lunch or dinner, invite everyone present to place their phones on the table, face down. The first one that picks up and faces their phone pays!

Our role is our state of mind according to our present environment. This role is the interface through which communication flows. When it is important to you to have a clear and open conversation with someone, come from your natural self as much as possible, within the boundaries of your role. This way there will be minimal distortion of the information you receive and perceive.

The person you have the conversation with also comes from his or her role, so initial communication will reflect that. To dig a little deeper, we have to encourage the other person to open up a bit more and qualify what they are saying. Initially, especially if this person is not used to have open and frank conversations with you, you may find some resistance to this process. You will get many forms of "I don't know" or "I am not sure." It may take a few attempts to engage a person in this way. Sometimes you may run into people who simply refuse to engage on a deeper level. Depending on the scenario you may persist for a while but at some point you have to either accept the unwilling 'participant' as they are, or release him or her back into the wild.

If you are passionate about living life from your natural self and being free from depending on external factors to fuel your contentment, you most likely wish this kind of living for the people you love and the people you work with. In other words, those who are sharing part, or most, of your journey with you. Just because you have newfound clarity from a natural self perspective, does not mean everyone around you will immediately adapt to your new ways. This will take some time, so be patient. See what you can do to encourage and inspire them to show up in their life roles more authentically.

This way you are going to have more meaningful conversations. Meaningful conversations do not equal deep and heavy conversations. What makes a conversation meaningful is its enhancement of contentment for those involved, and perhaps even the wider world. So this could mean to have that conversation you have been avoiding for some time, or, to have a light chat with a coworker about the weather. Now, a bit of light chitchat is probably not too much of a problem for you so let's focus on the more creative and constructive conversations that enhance the shared reality for those involved.

Initially your conversation partner will communicate from their role identified level. Some people are more open and share their point of view naturally, some people need a bit of encouragement. The way to do this is by the application of what I call *listening language*.

Listening language is a way of responding to someone's story in a non-intrusive manner. By using a form of language that avoids interjecting new content, opinions, and advice, the conversation partner's story comes purely from their own perspective. Our worlds are not flat and neither are our stories. Our stories are like our planet, spinning and including an atmosphere, a space in between, a solidified surface level, a deeper moldable level, and a solid core. All this is wrapped in consciousness from which all angles of perception are possible. To see what you cannot see right now, you need some change of perspective while exploring your story from core to atmosphere.

The more you are able to stay in your own story, the more hidden and subconscious information can emerge to the surface. Earlier in this book you have already been introduced to a language form which digs just that little deeper.

There are many types of questions which facilitate the story perspective to stay active without interjection. By not giving advice, opinion, or feeding back your interpretation of the story, you are keeping the story going without becoming a cowriter. It is the counter reality of a normal conversation, and it takes years to become highly skillful in the art of using these kind of techniques from a coaching and therapy perspective. However, there are a range of simple applications of *listening language* that enhance honest, open, meaningful conversations.

This is the territory where shifts happen and 'shift happens.' Mostly for the person relaying the story, and don't be surprised to experience some pleasant side effects if you facilitate the emergence of deeper knowing of the storyteller.

Remember the story is 'the end of the line' version. It is solidified with reason, retrospect, interpretation, and justification. The more the storyteller's contentment is dependent on this version of the truth, the more solidified it will be. A very solidified story is mostly wrapped in layers of 'I don't know' and 'I do not understand.'

This is the point where the storyteller seeks affirmation, confirmation, and / or advice that does the same.

Rather than giving suggestions, advice, or even pushing the same question on the person, a gentle way of getting a little deeper is to ask; "If you would know, what would it be?" "If you would understand, what would you know?"

Listening language in a non-intrusive way is a feeding back kind of conversation. People often describe things to clarify their point of view. The description can be further explored by a value-assigning question.

In the role model exercise you will have noticed such a value assigning question 'What kind of . . . is that?' This question gives further information beyond the well established opinion. When a situation is compared to something like; "It was like being hit by a bus" you can explore the context of that conclusion by asking; 'And when it is like that, (pause) it is like. . . what?'

Note that I have used 'that' and 'what' as indicators to more information. To someone unfamiliar with such content free language this may appear strange. To start this style of communication you can repeat some of the key information given by your conversation partner more freely; 'What is it like, feeling like you were hit by a bus?' This encourages your conversation partner to become more descriptive, and by doing so, new insights may occur to him or her. When the answer reveals further metaphorical language you can inquire with 'what kind of' or 'what type of' or 'what else.'

When you gently introduce this kind of language into your conversations with people you will notice how they start to self-fix, and self-problem-solve. You will start to see more of the person rather than their usual role position they take with you. You will be surprised by how inspired people feel, and how good people feel when they have conversations like this. It is a role changing kind of conversation, and as it does so, inevitably changes the wider environment to which all other roles correlate by influencing the shared reality. This subtle change in the shared reality can then already be perceived from your natural self. You will sense the shift in energy and will have a response like a sense, or instinct, or gut vibe.

To the 'facts and figures' mind the subtle changes are imperceptible, until it suddenly passes the tipping points of individual perspectives. In turn they create a tipping point in the role's environment and suddenly change is perceived by most. Which changes their behaviour as people respond to how things seem to them. The change in behaviour continues the wave of change into other roles and the wider community.

Changing the world really starts by changing just the one perspective. By staying connected to (or by mostly being) your natural self, you are one of the first that senses these kind of changes. Continuously adapt with this gradual process and you will never be presented with a whopping surprise. Choosing not to adapt gradually only means you will have to adapt suddenly and drastically at some point. Staying present in your natural self state not only enables you pick up all the subtle shifts, but you also facilitate the people in your environment to reveal more of their natural true self in the role state they are in.

This alone will make people respond more authentically - because people respond to the 'why' naturally and instinctively, even before becoming consciously aware of it. When you sense the urge to take over the conversation, interject your opinion, rescue, help, or be the expert person that knows better: gently self inquire what kind of you wants to do this. You will find this urge belonging to one or more of your roles.

In the next chapter you will find an exercise that optimises your perspective on issues, obstacles, or things you want to address. Try to self inquire the kind of expert, rescuer, or controller urges with that.

Endeavour to listen by leaving your knowledge and experience out of the conversation. You may be asked for your opinion by your conversation partner, especially if you have been prone to offering people your opinion and advice in the past. If that happens simply pass the question back to them and emphasize you are really interested in what they think about it all.

Remember when you are served with an "I don't know" kind of response ask; 'If you did know, what would it be?' or 'What would an expert advise us?' Please note people take some time to adjust. The first few times you have a conversation in the meaningful style you may not get a wholly participating conversation partner. Give your conversational partners time and several opportunities to engage.

People who speak similarly tend to have a similar belief system. This usually creates a sense of trust and feelings of being at ease. If you are in a scenario where you need to adapt from your natural self state drastically: start with style matching your conversation.

Avoid copying intonation and body language, this is so counterproductive I would almost suggest doing the opposite. You style match by speaking on the same level of intellect and word choice. Match the variety of words chosen. Avoid using the same words though, instead use similar words, and interject them at a similar frequency. In recent studies of speed dating conversations, they compared how people rated their dates. They particularly studied how this related to the type of language used between them. They found that the degree to which the language matched, correlated with how much they liked that particular person. Interestingly enough it is not just the style of language that does this.

The kind of pronouns used, and the degree to which they appear in different contexts, also heavily influences how connected people feel.

Speak what you normally leave unsaid: to yourself and to others. It takes bravery, but it defeats the undesired and enforces change. Admittedly this is a bit scary at first. It gets more challenging the closer the matter is to your heart.

Sometimes (often) you may deem it better not to ask for what you really want. The truth could blow up the needs, wants, hopes, and dreams. Take the risk though, undesired outcomes may truly serve you. If anything, at least it opens up bandwidth on all levels for new opportunities. Remember that eventually the dream will pop if that is what it means to do, and when it does so, the shock is going to be larger. Your bravery may even get rewarded as simply outright speaking the unsaid may solve a problem that otherwise would have festered into something ugly. You may get what you otherwise wouldn't have had. Ask your conversation partner to speak the unsaid. 'Talk to me as if I am someone who hears your inner voice.'

People have a strong instinctive sense that guides them, even if they are not very aware of it. If you have an agenda, or are not rooted in your natural self, your conversation partner will resist speaking freely. Only from the natural self you are open enough to hear and listen without judgment of character. This is not some altruistic encouragement by the way. I mean quite the opposite to selflessness; that from your natural self you are contentment independent, thus free and open to new perspectives, and hence, new opportunities. Because you are this independent, people in your environment will feel free to share their perspectives open and honestly.

This only enhances their own natural self in their roles so in the end everyone wins, creating true altruism.

When I speak of saying the unsaid to yourself, this is the kind of question you should ask yourself sometimes:

'What are you knowing and avoiding?'

'What is it that you assume not to know?'

Note this is a fairly confrontational question only to be asked with a pure heart. Especially when you ask someone else. In the context of a meaningful conversation and non-intrusive *listening language,* this kind of question only suits a well established meaningful conversation relationship, where trust is high, regardless whether this is in a personal, or a professional context.

A Problem Seen...
Is a Problem Solved

Simply by naming a problem, or by speaking out loud that which you normally leave unsaid, you add something to the shared reality field. This leads to inevitable change. It is that easy indeed. When there is a deeper underlying reason for a problem, start by finding a new perspective. Doing so will reveal enough information to name the problem correctly. Because a problem named is a only a problem solved when you name it correctly. The true name has an intrinsic relation to its essence. You do not need to understand where things have come from. There is no need to delve into the past and stir up old emotions. Frankly that kind of 'therapeutic fixing' is a waste of time and energy. What are you going to find out that you didn't know before?

Are you expecting the same track leads somewhere else altogether this time? Maybe it does so on the surface, but its authentic essence remains hidden. When the true enough name for the problem is not found you are only reinforcing it. How? Because you may eradicate 90% of the problem but you are not dissolving its roots. Like weeds they will grow back bigger and stronger if you leave the root in.

With matters of the mind, or even physical disease, what is left behind uncured is the strongest part. Subsequently this will invade the space you have created by eradicating the weaker 90%. You have effectively created an environment for the strongest most potent part of the root to adapt, evolve and thrive. Hence the importance of accurately naming the root-problem, without mucking about in past manifestations of it. Accurate naming means exposing its intrinsic values. Name the problem by its true nature and you kill it with a single strike to its root, heart, and source. Often we do know the true name of things. The true reasons why, and the true 'why' and 'why nots.' It is surprising how unwilling we are sometimes to admit what we already know. Instead, we seem to prefer ignoring it. Ignorance avoids invoking change, because change brings the unknown.

We are equally afraid of loss and gain. Act without fear of loss and gain because whatever it is, your happiness does not depend on what you are losing or gaining. The more role identified we are, the more we fear change - as we have too much of a dependency on this role's future existence. Even though we can hardly predict the outcome of change, our actions today are influenced by what we think may happen next.

Remember your natural self is based on your strong self. This has a stable sense of self and a steady source of happiness, contentment, and sense of security. By enhancing your roles from your natural self state, you are very well equipped to deal with change. Coming from your natural self not only enables you to correctly name problems, it also sets you up for enjoying the implications of invoked change.

By naming something by its true name, and done so with a pure heart from your natural self, it becomes part of the shared reality environment, and therefore, will invoke change. Hence a problem named is a problem solved. In folklore knowledge of a true name allows you to magically affect a person or being. Bilbo Baggins in the Hobbit knows not to reveal his real name to the dragon, as this would give the dragon advantageous power. In older stories the idea of knowing an entity's real name will defeat it. In the Brothers Grimm Rumpelstiltskin, the queen frees her firstborn child from the supernatural creature by learning his true name. A true name is a name which is identical to its true nature. The true name is the true nature, and thus the true life force. Without a true name, there are no roots that are grounded to receive the life force. Similarly, beliefs around faeries stealing unbaptised children are rooted from their unnamed state.

Naming something by its true name gives you the power to dissolve its life force. So the folklore and stories point to understanding the true nature of things and folk. Knowing the intrinsic of something gives you the power to enhance or dissolve its life force. Likewise for knowing your own true name, for that means knowing your true nature, knowing your natural self.

You now have control over your life force, and are free from any dependencies you may have created by becoming too much dependent on - or identified with - your role(s).

Magic happens when we meet in our natural state. Imagine how powerful and wonderful that life force may fuel activity in that environment. This is true in teams, businesses, organisations, friend groups, family, community, nations, and universes.

A problem named is a problem solved, facing your stuff, grabbing the bull by its horns, you name it, and it will involve saying the previously unsaid. Sometimes, by the very nature of things being unsaid, they seem to be somewhat hidden in parts of our knowing. We do not shine our lights on it too often, or not at all. Now you know your true nature better you are better equipped to find the true nature, and, the true name of things that may be blocking or limiting your aspirations.

To free your self from these issues and obstacles we have to look a little deeper: find a new perspective. After all, if you would know the true name, the true nature of the obstacle or issue, it would no longer exist by virtue of a problem named is a problem solved. To get a new perspective let's explore the following exercise: It is designed to find what part of your role(s) is casting a shadow over this true identity. You can use this model to solve problems, or to find new ways of being to achieve goals.

Describe your issue/obstacle.
Represent this in some kind of form on paper: write, draw, and / or doodle.

Ask yourself what you know about this. Ask this until you have no more answers.
If you get an "I don't know" response: inquire further with 'If I would know, what would it be?'.

Write, draw, or represent all your answers.

Now place these notes somewhere in the space around you. Take a position, in relation to these notes, that feels right. Have a play with that. It may be near, it may be far, it may be in another angle, it may be at a different height. Once you feel you and 'your issue' are in the right place, visualise your problem is alive and has turned into a wise old creature (you can make this as exciting as you like).

Now ask yourself how this creature perceives you. What does this creature know about you? What do you, and all you have done about this issue, look like from the perspective of the creature? Treat the "I don't know" like before. Gently ask yourself what else this creature knows about you and your issue or obstacle until no further information comes up.

Summarize your new understanding of your issue/obstacle. Which role area could this have come from? What was it in that role (or combination of them) that made that role like this? What else is in that role that reinforces this?

How does this role need to adapt? What needs to happen in the context and environment of that role? How does this relate to your natural self state?

What would happen if this role has changed?

What would happen if the context of this role has changed? What else would happen?

What is the most important thing you have to do now?

How can you do this by coming mostly from your natural self?

When are you going to do this?

Love & Relationships

"Never underestimate the capacity for romance, no matter the circumstance."

Why, if one has the eternal source of contentment and happiness within, should we seek connections of joy with anything or anyone? When you are in your natural self state, and have the clearest channel and connection to the inner source of contentment, you have everything you need to maintain peace of mind and general well-being. You are free to form connections to anything external, it being; ideas, status, objects, and relationships with others, without having to depend on that channel for your happiness, contentment, peace of mind, and, well-being. When you have no need, you are capable to fully enjoy external stimuli. When you have no feel-good-dependency on someone's love, you are worthy, and trustworthy, with the task of looking after their heart.

The richness, brightness, and vastness of the love between people depends on how much they have merged their true life force. When both partners spark and connect in their true name, their true essence, and their true natural self, there is nothing that stops them from thriving in their relationship. Owing to their ability to be free from feel-good-dependency, their love is connected at a level where the change and pace of life does not have any real impact on the quality of the relationship. Add to that the freedom of feel-good-dependency both partners have relating to their roles, status, ideas, and objects, and you have the strongest and most responsive relationship foundation you can ever have.

The brightness of the spark depends on how well matched the natural self essence of the partners are.

This celebration of reciprocality depends on how well one natural essence compliments the other. This is best explained in a model of space and momentum.

Human perception measures, or I should say; observes, the world in a spectrum of momentum (or time) and space. When you look around you right now, you see things tangible, solid, things that give shape to the space in which you are present. Simultaneously you sense things moving in this space, and if nothing appears to move you always have a sense of time (momentum). When we think of things in the past or the future we create these thoughts in compositions of space and momentum.

At some level everything is momentum you may say, and perhaps it is a question of density, but as we observe from the physical reality of our bodies let's say there is a tipping point that differentiates between the tangible space and the noticeable momentum. Everything in our universe is both, but may appear more one or the other.

As humans, we appear to have a preference in our personalities to be more like space, or to be more like momentum. For the sake of my models, I wish to point out that a model is a tool to clarify perspective and: every living soul has the capacity to assume any combination of both space and momentum in its expression. However, most people find their natural inclinations, and their natural preferences to be mostly at ease when identified with a certain balance of space and momentum. Obviously, as we can see in nature, certain spaces suit certain momentum expressions better than others.

It is on the level of this 'space-momentum-fit' that determines how well connected two people are. Similar preferences make great friends, and great partnerships. Reciprocal preferences make great love and lust connections. The model and spectrum of reciprocality is easiest explained in a simplified representation of opposites.

Obviously this two dimensional representation is lacking depth, and the true representation of the complexity of reciprocality and relationships is better explained in the shape of a sphere. A spinning ball of energy with a variety of different flavours and colours that represent the spectrum of space and momentum. In the linear model, we have on one end 'life,' the ever changing dance of motion and momentum, and on the other 'universe,' the space in which life happens.

Together they form the experience. You, me, and every other pronoun imaginable, is an expression of that experience. We are both life and the universe. There is a zone where the experience of individuality and perspective is at its most content and at peace. This zone will have various levels of mixtures between life and universe, depending on circumstances, all within its boundaries of contentment.

Love in relationships is experienced to the degree of reciprocality between the expression of individual natural essence. The higher the degree the brighter the spark, the intenser the fire of mixed life force. . . Here we are, we have now defined what it takes to have a truly great relationship. Well, err. . . I wish it was that easy. . . In essence I do believe this to be true. However, in today's world with countless role hats to wear, many people do not always authentically show up in their life(roles), and subsequently not always represent their natural self.

What happens if two people, heavily identified with their role(s) happen to be in each other's reciprocal role value? From their role induced perspective, the spark ignites the fire of romance, to the degree of reciprocality of the expression of their identified role self. Spark, 'whoosh,' ignition, passion, bang, boom, fireworks, sizzling into a relationship, which in time, grows apart at the same pace of their changing roles. Not always true I must say; if roles change accordingly for both partners in similar ways, and both are mostly subjected to similar circumstances, and therefore, experience the same kind of change, and their level and kind of identification with their role does not change, the relationship develops in a similar fashion for however long they maintain these kind of circumstances.

In these role identified connections the growing apart of relationships happens when partners become more identified with different aspects of their roles. As the nature of life is change, and roles change according to their circumstances, the way people adapt and develop may no longer have the same reciprocality as the relationship had at its origins. Circumstances are different, and how either partner has developed their identification with their roles, and the degree of that role identification, determines how clear the reciprocality channel is. It determines 'the level of spark.' If there is not enough oxygen to ignite the mutual fire it slowly dwindles.

People that have a certain level of 'feel-good-dependency' on their role, subsequently have a certain level of dependency on its circumstances. The partner is a huge part of those circumstances. When we are mostly identified with our roles, we fight for their survival as if we are trying to stay alive. This is the reason people stay in uninspiring jobs and relationships. The role perspective endeavors to keep its environment similar to its survival (comfort) zone. When a huge part of the role's environment changes (or when it appears to have changed hugely because change happens imperceptibly and gradually, and then appears suddenly), the person mostly identified with that role will try everything in his or her power to change those circumstances back to where it reciprocally sparked and ignited the fire of 'love.'

When things get tough this element of the relationship seeks solutions externally, first in changing behaviour, then in changing time spent together.

It often involves things like; 'if we do this and that, then it will get better' or 'if only he/she was like this/that, then...' -or- 'if only we were better off financially we wouldn't be in this situation.' Note that the common factor is a need to change the external circumstances of the relationship so to improve the quality of the internal love experienced. Often it is already too late, the mutual fire has dwindled, and so has the quality of the behaviour of both partners.

People respond to how things seem, and behave accordingly, leading to growing further apart. The interaction between the couple turns downhill because both have a feel-good-dependency on the mutual fire of love, and they feel less happy as time moves on. This will lead to a tipping point, appearing suddenly, but happening gradually.

Boom! The bomb goes off, blows up the unimportant stuff, and what is left is the moment of truth. A break happens instantly, or reconciliation is sought.

If the couple happens to be well enough matched on a natural self level, their relationship may be bumpy for some time, but it has a good chance to survive. They may find enough common ground to support each other's needs. When the couple sparked from the reciprocality that was present between their role selves at the time; and are not very compatible from a natural self perspective; the relationship most likely comes to an end. Either way, the relationship is a success because, in both cases, the old relationship has made space for a new one, which, as we have no choice but to evolve, may have a better foundation.

With the risk of being perceived as a hopeless romantic I believe that, in the beautiful world of love, the essence of a person is strong enough to guide loving connections, regardless whether or not someone knows themselves truly.

Most people instinctively assign more importance to how they feel about things when it comes to relationships.

Love and relationships are fine as long as people (mostly) obey their heart, and instinct. This is not only limited to love.

In life our natural essence shines through the perceived reality of the roles. Benefitting from this is merely a matter of clarity on, and refreshing the connection to, your natural state of self's preferences, values, and well-being zones.

Three Elements of Relationships

There are three elements in relationships. All relationships have the ability to fully embrace each element, but how much each element influences the relationship correlates to how much each partner is connected to their natural state of self. However, even when both partners are totally in tune with their natural essence, their relationship still goes through these element stages:

1. The need and dependency stage;

2. The partnership stage;

3. The unconditional stage.

The relationship, at any stage will be a mix of these three elements, each component will be present. None of these components are good, bad, better, or worse.

They are all valid and necessary requirements to form whole and balanced relationships. To what extent each component is present depends on the partner's compatibility, and of course, circumstance. If each component had its own colour, the level of each would compose the colour-state of the relationship at that moment.

Every relationship has these three elements, and each element could shine to a certain extent. If the relationship would be a transparent sphere, we could see the state of the relationship like a ball of light. Let's say the partnership element is orange, imagine our relationship sphere is mostly orange when we are dealing with finances, the colour of the new kitchen, and what kind of house we would like to live in. The colour of our sphere would signal the 'tone' of our relationship in that present moment. There will always be a level of orange with a mixture of the other two elements. The partnership element is always present. During times of play we will see more of the other elements. The need and dependency element of a relationship starts with that infatuation / honeymoon period and then settles into a period where an actual relationship forms. Partners in their natural essence state find their initial balance of how they like to give and receive their love. It is a dance of extended courtship that sets the tone and flavour of the relationship. These are the starting conditions.

In nature, we reap what we sow, and relationships are no different. The need and dependency element influences how excited we are to see each other, and how good we make each other feel. This is true for all, regardless how dependent for happiness on this you end up being.

When people are very role dependent, their relationships always carry a large element of this first stage dependency. It is not that role dependent folk have diminished their natural self essence, but they are simply not tuned into its signals. Like a detuned radio they are mostly listening to 'other' channels. The natural essence will have launched a full scale sensory overload campaign of 'I feel it in my water,' 'gut feeling,' and 'instinctive nudges' that have, at times, overruled the 'other' channels. However, there is a difference between listening to those senses and giving those senses a veto right. As role dependent folk take a very rational kind of approach to most things in life, they may have taken their gut feeling into consideration but assigned less weight to it in their decision making process. It all depends on having enough capacity of the emotional and thought bandwidth.

Comparing 'partner selection' somewhat crudely to 'buying things' we have all, at times, bought (into) something we actually did not really want. If we would have had the time and space to understand how we really felt about buying it, we would have left it on the shelf. And, depending on where on the road of life you are presently, most will have a similar story relating to romance. In the end of the day, as long as you are mostly natural self, and you follow your heart, whatever happens, your relationship roles will thrive. Circumstances permitting, I know, it takes two to have a good boogie, but even if things are temporary, and in the end even the longest relationship is, it still means you create a better relationship self/role for the next. Remember, love always returns to the heart and mind, even to the most role dependent person in the world.

Given enough time and experience relationships start to build the second element; the partnership. Friends, buddies, partners in crime, you name it; all the same to me.

Of course you are going to be best buddies, best mates, best of friends. And if you are not, wake up; you are in a 'self created neediness and codependency prison,' not a relationship. Where the need and dependency element outlines the starting conditions, the partnership element is the foundation built within the boundaries of these starting conditions. This foundation is literally what supports the 'relationship house' as a whole. Strong and suitable foundations according to its starting conditions as it were. You have to have the right kind of foundation, matching the requirements of the external grounds. If you have the wrong kind of foundation, subsidence may be the source of substantial damage. The partnership element is how we are when we are operating as the team. The 'ongoings' of daily life mostly. What makes it a relationship more than a partnership is how the other elements of need and dependency, as well as the unconditional element, are expressed in the play of sex and love.

The unconditional element of the relationship is the most adaptable as it is based on unconditional love. This kind of love is just for the other person, as they are, not what they represent in their roles. This element in the relationship does not mind what car someone drives, how much money they earn, and what kind of work status they might have. When the going gets tough the partners in the relationship turn to each other and to their love. It is love in the sense of how 'being in the relationship' enhances the natural state of contentment.

While the expression of each partner's roles may change, it does not change their relationship as they unconditionally accept each other as they are. These relationships have a limitless source of support, appreciation, and gratitude.

When we look at relationships as an 'at-one-ment' with each other, the need and dependency element is like the weak self - being too identified with the role status, and too dependent on it for individual happiness. The relating is therefore also weak. Partners have too much vested interested in the relationship relating to their own happiness. Sexually this kind of weak-self-relationship is also based on neediness. Often partners are mostly focussed on self pleasure, and less concerned about the experience of their partner. This may be true for the relationship as a whole. Providing the relationship mimics the starting conditions, the level of sexual reciprocality is stimulated mostly by external conditions such as; location, alcohol and other 'intoxicators,' dinner and other dating scenarios. Certain conditions need to be present to open the sexual attraction channel. The sexual expression has an underlying goal, is often self serving, and result driven.

The partnership element of a relationship is always there, it is the 'permanent,' and the least changing part of the relationship. It is where the relationship is in balance and is, therefore, like the strong self. This is a very self reliant, and self regenerating element. When the partnership element is strongest there is little bandwidth for sexual energy to flow. Sexual energy requires reciprocality, induced by external and internal stimuli. It is vital to pay attention to your sexual reciprocality channel. How clear is it? Are you fully comfortable in your own natural self state?

If you have a personal issue which affects your confidence and self belief, note that not everything has to be shared within the partnership.

When something is going on for you, which may affect how your partner sees you (people respond to how things seem) you may want to work on this intimate issue yourself, and enlist the help of trusted friends and family. I know some people feel everything should be out in the open in a relationship, all I am saying is to have a quick think about how this 'something' may affect how your partner sees you. Sexual polarity is a wonderful game you can play out in a universe of loyalty and trust. Be what you need to be in life's roles, so the partnership stays strong. Create the space for relaxing into your essence, and allow yourself to express yourself passionately in your work and leisure roles. When partners do not rely on each other for happiness, they set each other free. It is this kind of freedom which creates the unconditional bond. The unconditional element of relationships is the strong self stepping back into its role defined space and wholly enjoy and appreciate the other person for who she, or he, naturally is. It is the natural self version of the relationship. Being mostly self reliant for feeling contented, partners in the unconditional relationship have the freedom of play. People in these relationships literally play together, enjoy each other's love fully, and embrace time with each other as a gift.

They freely live in each other's hearts. The unconditional lover flows with the rhythm of their partner, capable of adapting to each other's deepest desires owing to their ability to deeply feel the other person. Sexually this fusion of each other's essence is sensual, and pleasure is focussed on the wanting, not needing.

Couples where this element is strongest have less dependency on external stimuli like romantic dinners, 'intoxicators,' or other things to be present.

When they are, they are an enhancement of the sexual experience, not a necessity to open the channel. They are creative and spontaneous, and understand sexual desire comes in waves. Like the moon, it waxes and wanes. Sexual polarity is high as the unconditional couple leave each other free to express their passion in their working and leisure life. Well-matched naturally inclined authentic creatures do have, at a deeper level, a relationship based on partnership and unconditionality.

All relationships are a mix of partnership with elements of need / dependence and unconditionalness. To what degree each element is present varies, and when so, is context driven. There may be certain circumstances where there is a greater neediness and dependency. The presence of an ex partner, being in a foreign or new situation, or simply being in an airplane, can affect the mix of these elements at any given time.

How to Have More Upsides

People change they say. I say our roles change and our deeper authentic self evolves. We all have fundamental preferences and values around things. Without them, we would not be 'ourselves.'

It is these preferences and values we cannot compromise for anything or anyone without experiencing a sense of loss and discomfort. Compromise on this fundamental level and you diminish your own ability to self-heal and self-generate contentment. At some point we all made compromises to less important values and preferences, just to make our life roles work. Circumstances change and we get stuck with ways of being which are less authentic and natural. We build on this change, unaware of these subtle changes as change happens gradually.

We keep chipping away at our preferences until we hit the barrier of 'to here and no further.' Chances are you have become rather identified with the role because of its attachment to its circumstances. Adapting to circumstances is great obviously, but only if you do not permanently compromise your natural preferred values. Note I say permanently, a little while for the sake of achieving tasks is fine.

Always remember why you are doing things, just to ensure you are not losing sight of the greater good of contentment. Sometimes life requires you to go against your natural inclined preferences. When it does, do not lose sight of 'why you are doing this' and there is little you cannot achieve.

It is when we consistently 'violate' our deeper values that we drain our energy. This is dangerous territory as prolonged or chronic compromise may affect the connection with your natural self. You effectively allow less bandwidth for the natural self's signals to reach your conscious thinking and emotional state. You can literally numb yourself and gradually detune, getting out of sync. Hence the value of knowing your deeper essence, your authentic natural preferences. When you have become too role identified you miss your instinctive signals. Subsequently, you are less aware of ongoing change in your surroundings. So change appears suddenly.

The natural self changes more at the pace of gradual change. The natural self is free, and so finds any sudden change less challenging. Life from the natural self seems more chaotic because change is 'more perceivable.' It certainly is more up and down. There is not much sameness and routine.

This may give the impression that life is unreliable. But the natural self relies on your own capacity for contentment.

By being free from attachment to work, money, objects, and relationships, the natural self is actually really reliable. It is the role self (which appears to be reliable and steady) that is unreliable in the end because everything external changes, and ends. The natural self is open to small changes and the small stressors; hence appearing to live life more randomly, but as life itself is random it is very stable indeed.

This is why the natural self thrives, because it changes its roles faster and more effectively than a person who is too attached to the joy of the external role and its status, ideas, and objects.

Mind Wandering

Scientific research has linked mind wandering, (in other words; thinking away and not focussed on whatever you are doing) to experiencing unhappiness. We are significantly happier when we are present. Here and now. People on average mind wander 30% of the time. When at work people mind wander 50%, and 10% of folk mind wander when they are making love. When we do mind wander and think away about pleasant things we are only slightly less happy (I am sure this must be the majority of that 10%). When we think about neutral things we become much more unhappy, and this increases significantly when we mind wander about negative things.

The quality and volume of data shows that mind wandering precedes unhappiness, not the other way around.

When the mind wanders, happiness loses, especially when our minds wander into our fears and anxieties.

Fear; The Story of What Will Happen Next

Worries and fears are stories of what will happen next. Stories with outcomes we wish to avoid. They have a thought-beginning, a what-happens-next-middle, and a this-is-what-it-will-come-to-ending. The 'what will happen next' is an anticipated thought story based on how one thing may affect the other. Most of this kind of thinking leaves very little space for alternative, random input that could affect the outcomes. Instead, we seem to think we understand our future.

The future always carries an element of randomness. To ignore the possibility of alternative outcomes is in direct conflict with the natural world. When the mind is made up and is certain that something undesired is going to happen, the body communicates with stress and anxiety. Not because of the 'certain' undesired though. That underlying feeling is signaling that you have excluded too many other possibilities. Your focus is too narrow, your bandwidth too narrow. At this point instinct takes over and we put ourselves on high alert: it is our natural response to be ready for the unexpected. This natural stress reaction state enables us for fight or flight, and physically prepares to heal wounds faster. It also activates our deeper more instinctive brain, and reason and rationale are certainly in short supply. Good for real life threats, not so good for imagined ones.

When we are identified with our roles, our stories are limited to the boundaries of the role's world (view). When you are mostly identified with the natural self you are less limited by these boundaries of the role-worlds. The natural self's boundaries are flexible, adaptable, and only limited by preferences. This is a great property of the natural self, and the driving force of your ability to thrive in times of change (life always changes). Being more open to randomness and unexpected outcomes naturally means less anxiety and stress.

Having a vested interest in something which has yet to happen is bound to create a fear of loss - even though this is utterly ludicrous as the event of losing it may show your dependency was nothing but a limitation to you. Our shared realities have many emotional markers attached to scenarios and circumstances. Remember most people have learned to identify with their roles in life and are mostly unaware of these markers. Having said that, almost everyone can feel 'the tension in the room' when you walk into a space where there has just been an argument. However many have unwillingly suppressed the vital and useful information the anxiety story has.

For those living in the present natural state these subtleties are more tangible, and the more one obeys the little nudges, inklings, and hunches, the more fine-tuned this skill becomes.

When life was less complex, the evolution of man made it possible to learn from the mistakes or errors made by other members of our species. Evolution dictates what smells attractive, and what does not. So an energetic field of anxiety around a poisonous food or dangerous animal is very useful to pick up. Note these are energetic signals without words, so as a natural authentic human being you are present enough to sense other people's energy markers in our world. It is a good skill to have, and you can see how this kind of sensing works in the animal kingdom in relation to navigating to breeding grounds, watering holes, and food sources.

In today's society things are wildly more complex. There are many different kinds of energetic markers in our field, most of them generated by folk who are mostly identified with their roles. These markers are unimportant. Just like being attached to the external for your happiness is not clever, taking on the irrelevant worries and fears from the external is mostly pretty useless too. To those who have a happiness interdependency on status and objects, emotional markers around the age and model of your car are important. Then you better worry about not having the best looking, latest, most impressive model, right? All these emotional markers are around you all the time.

In your natural self state you have to filter through all the noise you receive and deem which signals are important and useful, and which are not. Some fears are useful, like the one you feel on the edge of a cliff for instance. . . This is a very natural information marker you have taken on through the evolution of mankind. In this case you have benefited nicely from the errors of previous generations. The emotional energetic markers in our world, however they are created, either by your own experience, or that from others, correlate to a kind of thinking. It radiates from our sensory receptors to our cognitive filters and results in thoughts made up from words and imaginary pictures and moving image. Being in the natural self state gives you the bandwidth to process this information correctly. You may mistake a shadow for a wolf, but never a wolf for a shadow. It is all about understanding the vitality of the signals and markers in our surroundings.

The clearer your natural self channel, the less mistaking wolves for shadows.

In 'The story of what will happen next?' we interject a quick response that assigns these kind of values. The below is a very useful way to proactively improve the clarity of the natural thinking channel.

How likely is it, that the kind of thinking you are experiencing, is going to happen? And if you deem it likely, . . . could there be a possibility, . . . even remotely, . . . that it would not happen this way? If so, determine in what kind of circumstances this would have different possible outcomes.

How 'true' is this kind of thinking? Have you really perceived this right? Is there, . . . however remote, . . . a chance it may not be true? And; if so, what kind of circumstances would it take, for this not to be true?

How useful is this kind of thinking? Is this useful to enhance your happiness and joy you self-generate? Or is this an external happiness source? How useful is it to your natural self state to have this kind of thinking? Does it serve your essence and your 'why you do things'?

Is there a reward for this kind of thinking? Like; if I don't touch that snake it will live? Some rewards are payoffs that keep certain roles alive. Are you keeping unwanted roles, or unwanted aspects of your role, alive?

Is this kind of thinking important? When you detect it has some external happiness dependency, simply deem it 'not important.' Is this kind of thinking important when you are in your final hours? When it is not, it is 'not important!' This is a powerful label as the level of importance determines the level of openness to experience the energetic charge that comes from this matter.

The rule of thumb for anxiety, resulting from your interpretation of your own storytelling, is this: When the anxiety is unnatural - 'the bigger the anxiety the less important the matter'. When the anxiety is natural (cliff edge, poisonous snake) - 'the bigger the anxiety, the more relevant the matter.'

How to make this beneficial in our role states? Simple: listen to the subtle anxieties and fears. Understand what that story is about with the use of the above.

Act on it. This way you are adapting your roles, and at some point you will pick up the gradual, usually imperceptible, subtleness of change.

Get Out of Your Own Way.

Getting out of your own way is simple. What is it you do that is stopping you from doing what you really want to do? I used to be a master at staying busy doing tasks or jobs that prevented me doing what I really wanted, or needed to do. You can spend much time working on your sales pitch, getting your website content 'just right', instead of getting out there and ask folk to buy your product. You can spend much time sorting out little problems, rather than starting with the 'biggie.' What about dealing with other people's problems instead of your own? When this looks familiar something is in the way. Now let me save you heaps of time; it is you. You could call it 'mindset,' but I still think that is you. For me, it's me, every time!

How do you get out of your own way? Easy, stop looking at yourself. Do not see yourself from a perspective which is outside of you, the perspective of the narrative. If you are not looking out from your own perspective ladies and gentlemen; you have left the building, not Elvis!

Notice when you judge yourself. Notice when you compare yourself. You are really looking from the outside in, then take some kind of position of judgment. Stop being your own judge, leave that to other people. Judging yourself, looking from the outside in, reinforces belief-systems that stopped your aspirations previously. Be brave, look from the inside out. Come from the deeper natural side, let the gut, heart, and instinct rule! Use reason to guide it, not the other way around. This way you are beaming a new kind of signal into the shared realities of your roles. Do this long enough and the world responds.

It is nature's way to evolve, and people respond mostly to 'why' you do things, and not to what you do. It is the 'why-drive' as I like to call it.

By mixing in new ingredients in the shared reality you have with others, the recipe changes and the food will taste different. A new thing has been created, and when there are new ingredients there is new opportunity.

What I mean is not like manifesting from a perspective of influence: what power hungry manipulative freak came up with that anyway?

No, this is evolution baby! Working with nature's way (change), and by doing so, driving its change.

Next time you see yourself from the outside in, have a little laugh at your own expense.

You can only fly with the winds of change when you are looking out of your own eyes with love.

You only have your own perspective, so stop pretending, stop judging.

Come back home, and if you do not know where that is; it is where the heart is remember?

Eye-Opener & Eye-Closer

Every day is a new day, and as change is imminent, open up your bandwidth for new opportunities. People are creatures of habit, and when too role-identified, will strive to keep things the same, do things in a similar way, and expect things to get done as usual. However, change happens gradually, and our tendency for inattentional blindness will hide subtle change from our perception when our minds are busy.

The more role dependent you are, the less bandwidth to properly weigh up the subtle notions of change, and the subtle notions of your deeper senses. In time, change does appear suddenly, and perhaps you have pretended not to notice, but when one day everything has changed there is a lot of catching up to do.

Advantageousness means to ride the wave of change, be with it, adjusting your perspective and movements along the way. Believe today will be like yesterday and today will be your 'Jesterday' - a bit of a joke really!

You are not only as good as your last performance, you are only as good as the boundaries of your beliefs. Be realistic enough not to expect to leap into progress. Change happens gradually, then suddenly. Align your natural self, your authentic preferences, beliefs, and values, and apply this to everything you do. The reality, which is the shared reality, will start to respond to the ripples of change you are sending into the world. In time the world answers accordingly.

Every day is new, look at the sky, it is a new piece of artwork. Start the day by making time to show up in your roles. Know where you are going, what you are doing, and who you are involving.

Address the most trickiest of tasks first, do what you can according to today's circumstances so you can pause it and focus on the remainder of tasks with all your thought, emotional, and instinctive bandwidth. With 'pausing' I mean to take the view that this task is ongoing, and you have done what is possible in today's circumstances. Get it to a point where you can pause it, even if that means you have done little more than determined that 'right now' or today is not the right time to address this matter.

When you pause a task, project, obligation, or something that weighs on you mind, imagine you temporarily place it on a shelf, ready for the right circumstances. This shelf is the 'task bar,' or 'library' with an automatic natural filing system. Do the same with anything that is occupying your thinking when you want to go to sleep. Place tasks and projects on you imaginary shelf, and trust your mind to file them where appropriate. When the circumstances require your 'paused-file' it will be immediately accessible.

When you are being kept awake by thinking about people, wish them a good night. I imagine they are going to bed, or home, or traveling away. When I say goodnight to them I 'see' them going to bed, or go to their bedroom, or go home, or go to their travel destination. 'Matching appropriate scenarios' is the right way of doing this. So imagining someone who you have a professional relationship with getting into bed does not match the ingredients of the relationship. You probably do not know what their bedroom looks like.

Whatever the nature of your thinking is, whatever keeps your mind too busy to log out, if you use the wrong context of saying good night, or good bye, you are not logging out of this particular thought pattern. What is important, is that the scene in which your 'goodnight/bye' is taking place matches the relationship you have with this person. When the person that keeps you awake like this is someone from work, a client, employee, or superior; imagine saying goodnight/bye to them in the context where they are going home. Either from your communal work space, or the way they travel home. See them leaving in their normal way of transport; car, bus, taxi, walk, underground and subways, whatever is applicable.

When this is a distance relationship; wish them a good night via the phone, skype, face-time, or equivalent. Your child may be on a school trip; imagine tucking your little one in, and say good night as you would have if you were there.

Someone you have taken a romantic shine to; imagine you are saying goodnight inside their home, and ensure you do this from the right place that reflects the level of intimacy this relationship already has. You can see how this can easily lead to another thought pattern. That may be a nice day dream, but it still keeps you logged in. It keeps the process alive, and this requires your life force to feed it. Your body responds by staying awake, ensuring you have the instinctive, emotional, and cognitive bandwidth to enhance your perspective. Saying goodnight/bye to people and filing your paused tasks allows you to log out of your mind occupying thinking.

When you have wished your good nights, sweet dreams, and filed your paused tasks, it is time to relax your body. Pay attention to your breathing. Breathe in through your nose, and out through your mouth. When you breathe in, imagine the air you breathe is filling your lungs like water pouring into a glass, touching the bottom and filling its way up to the top. Breathe in, relax and lightly push out your lower tummy. 'Belly button out' on the in-breath, 'belly button in' on the out-breath. Air filling your lungs from bottom to top. Breathe in through your nose, and out through your mouth when the breath 'touches' your throat.

Become aware of the little gentle muscles around your eyes, relax them, make them soft. Relax your mouth muscles, the back of your head, your neck and shoulders. Become aware of your shoulders, and move your attention through your arms to the tip of your fingers. Relax and soften your arms. Flow your attention back to your shoulders and bring it to the front of your neck. Relax your throat and move your relaxing attention down into your chest. Keep breathing deeply, as you feel the relaxing and softening of your body. Become aware of your solar plexus, and move further down into the lower tummy and your reproductive zone.

Now, become aware of your legs and move your attention to the tip of your toes, spreading the relaxation as you move back to your solar plexus.

Rest in your centre, your heart, and your essence.

A Story About a Way

All we have, is how we feel about ourselves, every single moment. Some level of grief is at the source when darker moods emerge. A kind of grief born from things not being the way we want, need, or feel entitled to have.

Ultimately everyone strives to be content. I believe this is a person's compelling drive. Ask 'why do you want this', 'or why do that' enough and sooner or later a word similar to contentment will emerge. Happiness, love, joy, fun, thrill, you name it, all the same to me.

Extreme sociopathic exceptions considered excluded (although at some level there must be a compelling drive for emotional peace) I consider 'happiness & contentment' the human modus operandi (MO). 'Happiness is the way.'

Everything is better when we are content, in fact; was it not a certain Lao Tzu (creator of the Tao Te Ching - 604 - 532 BC) who argued: *"There is no greater (human) disaster than not being content"*?

Life, Work, and Relationships are better when you feel good. I do, however, acknowledge what I called our MO just now to be a somewhat conscious approach. On a more fundamental instinctive level, our human MO - like any other natural creature - is to Thrive.

Modern lifestyle cultivates the sourcing of contentment and happiness mostly externally, creating a dependency on 'things' to stay as they are. And when they don't - and they don't - it is down to our emotional and mental capacity to create alternatives for feeling good. The contentment source lies within. I believe many of us waste tremendous emotional and mental energy in our external search for happiness. It is our nature to strive for being content so when our contentment mostly relies on other people, status, ideas, and objects we have become slaves to our context.

Much of our natural ability to thrive is lost by maintaining one's feel-good relationships, career status, ideas in your mind of what you think is good for you and others, and up-keeping worldly possessions.

With most of your energy serving your compelling drive to maintain feeling good this way, your conscious awareness of experiencing whatever is happening right now, and your ability to perform at tasks, is at best compromised. Not only do you not have your full emotional capacity available, the degree of energy needed for external happiness maintenance dictates how much presence of mind you have left to see more opportunity, to assume less, to listen better, and to enjoy whatever is in your environment right now.

In a digital context it is a matter of bandwidth; if you need most of your bandwidth to upkeep externally sourced contentment you do not have much time and space for creating, innovating, and emerging the new.

An old Asian proverb says; *'Once you do not need love, you are capable to love.'* I freely morph this to; *'Once you do not need the external for contentment, you are able to enjoy it.'*

It is simply so that life, work, and relationships are better when you do not rely on them for happiness, contentment, and, peace of mind. Only when you are self relying, self healing, and self generating contentment you can fully enjoy the external.

The art in life is to know yourself like your strong self and thrive in life by adapting to its changing nature. Where our strong self has a stable and permanent essence, our thriving natural self has an evolving and adjusting essence. It does so by being more present in the external world, however, instead of being led by a feel-good-dependency on outcomes, objects and people - like the weak self - the thriving self depends mostly on its own source for contentment, joy, love, and clarity of mind.

The Thriving Self is therefore free to morph to change because there is no need to keep circumstances the same to experience feeling good. It is that subtle difference in feel-good-dependency which makes the difference between having more upsides to downsides in life, careers, and relationships (change).

These days, my 'outside' attachments no longer need to bring me contentment, love, and joy: I am free because I self generate sufficient feel-good-factor.

This leaves me free to enjoy the attachments to my relationships, status, and worldly possessions without being bound by them as a source for wellbeing. I do not mean cultivating the ability to decathect from a person, idea, or object (withdraw one's feelings of attachment in anticipation of a future loss). What I speak of, as the thriving ability of the natural self, is simply knowing that love, happiness, and contentment, cannot be sourced from another person, an idea, or an object.

I am attached to others and their love for me, my status, my possessions, and my aspirations in a totally free way, open large bandwidth style. This is where life gets radical, sensational, and easy, because all the external joy is fully enjoyable in the moment. It is like oil on my fire while resting in the knowing I do not need the oil to keep my fire burning.

Life's events can rattle even the strongest of us, and when it does it is irrelevant what caused it. What is outrageously relevant is knowing that; you alone, have the innate ability to come out better, stronger, and shining like a sunny day in spring. I hope with my experience in designing life coaching and personal growth training methods I have been able to design a significant means of support to finding your own way to this beautiful essence of your mind.

The insight of the thriving self perspective is the essence of the material I teach, whether it is this book you are holding or any of my Surf Life Coach Adventure Sessions and Retreats. Whether you are happy as a pig in mud, or prone to sadness; this material enables you to live life with more upsides and 'design your life' by knowing what in you is changeable, and what is not.

May your life be full of love, laughter, and gratitude.

Be human, make errors, be open to love even if it means you are open to pain.

Be humble, it is the only way.

Life is like waves, the transfer of life energy, up and down, in a rolling elliptical pattern like planetary orbits around the sun.

Don't try to hold on to what is happening right there. Just go with the motion, keep riding it in your own unique style until it crashes on the shore where its energy takes on a different form.

You can't stop the wave, but you can learn how to surf it. . . or be tumbled around in the surge of the currents until the waves spit you out onto the sand, leaving you gasping for air, wondering how you got there.

You will never control the future, so you will never control the kind of waves coming your way. You can control how you deal with the future, it is up to you to ride the wave, or let the wave ride you.

Enjoy the Ride.

Life
Is
Like
The
Ocean.

Sometimes
Turbulent.
Sometimes
Serene.

Sometimes
Beautifully
Aligned.

No
Wave
Is
The
Same
And
There
Is
Always
Another
Wave.

You
Cannot
Stop
New
Waves
Reaching
Your
Shores.

Yet
You
Can
Learn
How
To
Surf.

Land-Life
Looks
Different
From
The
Ocean.

Surf
Your
Waves
Of
Change

. . .

Aloha